Study Right:
a simple guide to effective study

MANNY ASTON

REEDY
BOOKS

REEDY BOOKS PTY LTD
www.reedybooks.com

Copyright © Manny Aston, 2025

First published in 2006
Reprinted 2013
Revised edition 2025

National Library of Australia
Cataloguing-in-Publication data

Aston, Manny, 1961 - .
　　Study right: a simple guide to effective study.

　　Bibliography.
　　For tertiary students.

　　ISBN: 978- 0-9757241-3-2

　　1. Study skills – Handbooks, manuals, etc. I. Title.

　　371.30281

All rights reserved. No part of this publication may be reproduced, stored in a retrieval system, or transmitted in any form or by any means, electronic, mechanical, photocopying, recording or otherwise, without the prior permission of the publisher.

contents

contents iii
preface v
acknowledgements vi
1. the basics... 1
   why study?.. 1
   what to study 2
   where to study 3
   when to study 9
   how to study 10
2. organising your time 11
   organise yourself 11
   finding the time to study 16
   using the 'extra' time to study 19
3. in class 23
   attendance is the key 23
   preparing for class 25
   what to do in class 25
4. taking notes 29
   why take notes.. 29
   taking notes from a spoken source............ 31
   taking notes from a written source............ 33
   decide on a note-taking method 35
   note taking equipment 37
   what to do with your notes 39

5. retaining information 41
understanding your material: PQ4R 41
remembering your material........................47

6. written assignments 51
understanding the task 51
gathering information................................54
referencing 56
writing drafts 61
revising the drafts 64
presentation and layout 68

7. exams 71
types of exams 71
types of exam questions............................72
before the exam.......................................78
immediately before the exam 80
during the exam.......................................83
after the exam 85

8. the psychology of study 86
setting grade goals 86
coping with 'difficult' subjects......................87
dealing with stress 88
support networks 90
determination and persistence 92

references 93

preface

Study Right deals with a range of issues related to effective study including exam preparation, writing assignments and reports, time management, and dealing with study-related stress.

So often there is an easier way to approach a study task, a better method, a piece of advice that may give you an edge. These are highlighted throughout the book in sections called "tricks of the trade".

Students should find the suggestions in *Study Right* easy to follow and easy to apply. I hope that by using the book, you will discover the benefits in their results, and find the study experience to be a pleasurable and rewarding one.

Note on the revised edition.

It's hard to believe that it's been almost 20 years since this little book was first published. Much has changed in education in that time, but the basics still remain the same. I've resisted the temptation to rewrite everything, and have merely paid greater attention to the online environment.

See you in another 20 years. ☺

MA

acknowledgements

A body of work such as this is never completed in isolation. I owe a debt to other authors who have written on the subject of study, and have no doubt influenced my views and opinions. From the opening paragraph of a course study guide, to class handouts, to in depth books on study skills; all have no doubt played some part in this book.

What acknowledgement section would be complete without thanking one's Mum and Dad? Thanks also to my dear wife and three beautiful children. I can only hope that they find the joy of learning as rewarding as I do.

It of course goes without saying that my esteemed colleagues and the countless students I have taught over the years have provided the greatest motivation to complete a book such as this. My thanks to you all.

1. the basics

You can become a more effective student almost immediately, and the best place to start is with the basics: what to study; where to study; when to study; how to study; and making sure you consider *why* you are studying.

why study?

There are many reasons why people study. Perhaps you want to learn about an area in which you have a strong interest. Or maybe you have a particular career in mind. You might want a better job, change of career, or you might just want the intellectual stimulation.

Ultimately no single reason is better than another. The important part is that you remain motivated. If making your parents happy is enough of a reason to keep you motivated … then go for it. If the status gained by having the 'piece of paper' at the end of your course is all that matters to you … no problem.

As long as you are motivated to study – whatever the reason – you have every chance of success.

what to study

Once you are comfortable with *why* you are studying, the next logical step is to make sure you know exactly *what* is expected of you.

You will be expected to attend classes – either in person or online - and participate to the best of your ability. You will need to prepare assignments, essays and reports, and in many cases sit for examinations. You will also have to organise yourself in such a way that your assessments are submitted on time, and are of a sufficient standard to pass the subject.

Exactly what you will be studying will be communicated to you at the start of the semester, usually in a document called a Unit Outline, or Assessment Guide.

tricks of the trade
Read your unit guides thoroughly.
Read your unit guides thoroughly.
Read your unit guides thoroughly.
Believe me, it's worth repeating!

These guides will also include any set textbooks, and the topics you can expect to cover. Your teachers will often supply their own guide which should give you the specific dates each assignment is due, and at the very least a rough idea of the nature of each assessment event.

It is also important to know which units are prerequisites to other units, as that will determine how you allocate your time. For example it's best to put more emphasis on a core unit that is fundamental for your progress to the next semester.

where to study

Most of your study will take place in one of two environments: on-campus or off-campus. *On campus* is the school, college or university itself. *Off campus* is everywhere else – your room at home, the kitchen table, or the local library. Whatever the place, it is important to feel comfortable and familiar with where you study as people work far better in a familiar environment.

explore the campus

The trick to mastering your on-campus environment is to familiarise yourself with where everything is as quickly as possible. If you are new to a school or college, it's well worth doing some reconnaissance. For example it's a good idea to note places that might become important to you: student administration, parking, the canteen, the faculty office, teacher's offices, the main noticeboard, and so on. Make sure you have an up to date timetable listing your subjects, classrooms or lecture theatres. Also remember to physically go to your classrooms beforehand, so that you are not racing around searching at the last minute.

By the first week you should ensure you've paid all your fees, joined the library, organised your student ID card … in other words you should finalise all the niggly little administrative items that might interfere with your study once you're well into the semester.

join the student association

If you are studying outside of the school environment, it's almost certain your campus will have a Student Union or Student Association. It is an excellent idea to join – after all, their main goal is to support students. Membership usually entitles you to discounts for parking, photocopying, and has host of other benefits such as organised sporting and social activities.

use the library

Apart from your classroom, the library is probably where you will spend most of your study time. Find an area of the library that you feel comfortable in, and make that your regular study place. Don't get too attached to it, however, as sometimes the library can get crowded (particularly around exam time) and you may be forced to sit elsewhere!

The library is one of your most important resources. If you don't already know, you should learn how to find information and to look up references.

> **tricks of the trade**
> Most librarians are very helpful if you have any questions and many libraries offer 'Library Tours' during the early part of the semester. It's very worthwhile of your time to attend.

Don't ignore the magazines and periodicals sections, or the reference section. You also need to discover where the call-numbers are located in the library. Become familiar with the many online databases available.

find a study workspace

Most people seem to study best in a quiet room on their own, one which is well lit, and is at a reasonable temperature. Some people find that music in the background helps them to study. I like listening to music when completing routine tasks, but if I hear it while I study, my mind is on the tune, not the material I need to learn. Studying in front of the television is definitely not recommended!

You should try to create a set *place* for study. When I go out to my office, I'm immediately placed in study or work mode, after all, that's all I do when I'm out there. So creating a study workspace is certainly a big advantage.

The idea is to arrange the things around us to *help* rather than distract from study. This includes where you put things on your desk, accessibility of books, notes, papers and so on. To make your environment work for you, familiarity is important.

Your workspace should be comfortable, as you'll be spending quite a bit of time there, but not too comfortable – you're planning to work, remember, not relax.

> ***tricks of the trade***
> Delete all games off your computer – especially Solitaire. If possible, use another computer to put all the games on. ☺

Ideally, the lighting should be quite bright – fluorescent lights may not be the most attractive in terms of décor, but they are certainly practical in terms of visibility.

The room temperature should be mild, perhaps even on the cool side. A warm room is very cosy, but 'cosy' can equal 'sleepy'. On very hot days, air conditioning is a real bonus.

get the right equipment

The things you put in your workspace place are also important. Let's start with a good desk and a comfortable chair. Your desk should be roomy enough to fit a computer and some books, and still leave you space to write. A bookshelf and some sort of filing system like binders are also most useful. A computer with a reasonable word processing package is almost an essential item, as is a printer. Your budget and available finances will determine just how up to date your equipment will be.

You should equip yourself with a good general dictionary such as the Macquarie or *Australian Concise Oxford Dictionary*. Another useful reference is a thesaurus (a book of synonyms), which will help you to find alternative words and avoid constant repetition when writing assignments. *Roget's Thesaurus* is the best known of several on the market. A hard-copy dictionary and thesaurus will complement the computer-based versions nicely.

about textbooks

You will probably need to buy at least one textbook per subject – it will usually be in hard-copy or in e-book form. Some books are *set texts*, while others are *recommended* reading. A set text is usually one that is essential to the completion of the course, and so naturally it is advisable that you obtain it. Recommended texts are those which the course coordinator, or teacher feels would be beneficial to your understanding of the course, but are not essential to own.

Textbooks are very valuable educational tools … if they are read! There is no point in buying a textbook that is never opened. That, in study terms, is called a very expensive paperweight.

> ### tricks of the trade
> Look on college noticeboards for second hand textbooks for sale.

Second-hand textbooks are an excellent alternative when you are watching the budget, but make sure the book is in satisfactory condition and that you are buying the current edition. Sometimes older editions are acceptable, but it is best to check with your teacher. Page or chapter references may be given in class and it will be tiring to constantly translate page numbers from your friend's new edition textbook.

> ### tricks of the trade
> Build up a professional library by going to various book sales. Textbooks are often sold at drastically reduced prices because it is not the latest edition, or is over-ordered stock.

If you are considering photocopying a part of a textbook, do your sums first and compare the copying price with the price of buying the book. Often you'll find it's cheaper to simply buy the book, especially if you find it second-hand. Copyright laws usually allow you to copy or reproduce a maximum of 10 percent of the total number of pages for educational purposes – in other words, study or research.

when to study

The strategies of how to free up time to study will be discussed in the following chapter. What interests us here, is what time of day is the best time to study, and how long you should study for.

You can probably guess the answer: like so many aspects concerning study, "everybody is different." Some people work well late in the evening and even after midnight. Others seem to work better in the morning. All things being equal, our minds tend to be fresher in the morning after a good rest.

The golden rule when considering how *long* to study for is: it is not possible to study for long periods without a break. It is possible to *sit* for long periods without a break, but that is not study. Generally we are able to concentrate for between 45 minutes and 90 minutes. After that, you may find yourself staring blankly at a wall, or reading the same line over and over again.

That's the cue to have a short break. Have a cup of coffee, file some class notes, or organise your books. After the break, you can go back to studying refreshed. Be careful about extending the break indefinitely, though.

how to study

Attending classes, taking notes, writing essays, sitting for exams, retaining information, and the psychology behind study – are all part of the "how to study" experience. In fact, there is a lot you can do to increase your chances of success even before your first class. However, once the semester commences, there will be greater demands on your time. Managing that time effectively is what makes the difference between an average student, and an exceptional student.

2. organising your time

Managing time is almost as important a skill as study itself. A perfect assignment can lose points because it is submitted too late. The process of time management for students is quite simple. Firstly, organise yourself by determining what you have to do and when you have to do it by, then find the time to do it, and finally, in the words of a famous marketing slogan, "just do it"!

organise yourself

The job of organising your time is made a lot easier if you can organise yourself. This means sorting out all the material related to the course you are studying, and constructing a task-list of all your assessment events.

organise your material

It is very important to have a set place for your study material – 'study material' in this case refers to unit outlines, assessment guidelines, notes, handouts, class notes, photocopies you may make, and so on.

Loose notes and papers have a tendency to fall out of folders, have coffee tipped over them, or simply mysteriously disappear. One of the most useful items to organise your notes is a simple ring binder. The beauty of a ring binder is that you can move material around. Some students have a separate binder for each subject; others only carry notes they need for that day, or that week.

> **tricks of the trade**
> Make sure that you put your name and college name on your study material. If you lose it, there is at least a chance it will be returned.

Ultimately, you should use whichever method works best for you. What is important is that your notes are organised and easily accessible.

make a task-list

For each subject you attempt, there will undoubtedly be a series of assessment tasks. It is very important to have one document that lists all of those tasks in order of their due date – the semester *task-list*.

The best way to construct a task-list is to gather all necessary information, then combine and prioritise.

step 1: gather information

Most of the information you need to complete your task-list will be in the unit guides. These are an essential tool in establishing your study objectives. Generally a unit outline will have your teacher's contact details, learning objectives, a list of topics to be covered, a list of assessment tasks, due dates, and what percentage of the total mark each assessment is worth (the subject weighting).

So let's say you have two subjects in the semester, Marketing Principles and English Literature. In the Marketing subject there are two assessment events:

1. A report worth 80% of the subject mark, due on 27 May.
2. An in-class exam worth 20% of the subject mark, on 02 June

In the Literature subject there are four assessment events:

1. An assignment worth 10% of the subject mark, due on 26 March.
2. An assignment worth 10% of the subject mark, due on 16 April.
3. An in-class presentation worth 10% of the subject mark, due on 28 May.
4. An exam worth 70% of the subject mark, sometime in the exam period which will be between mid June to early July.

step 2: combine and prioritise

Combine all the assessment tasks for all the subjects, and then list them in order of the due date. Leave an extra column for the date you want to *finish* the assignment by.

Congratulations, the resulting table is your semester task-list. If possible, you should try to make your task-list fit on a single A4 page – this makes it easy to pin up on your noticeboard, or place in the front of your folder.

	TASK	%	DUE DATE	
			SUBMIT	FINISH BY
English Lit	Assignment 1	10 %	26 Mar	
English Lit	Assignment 2	10 %	16 Apr	
Marketing	Report	80 %	27 May	
English Lit	Presentation	10 %	28 May	
Marketing	Exam (class)	20 %	02 Jun	n/a
English Lit	Exam	70 %	Jun/Jul	n/a

Many students write each assignment into their diaries (which is a good thing to do), but will only realise an assessment is due when they open the diary for that week. Why not enter assignments into your student diary *and* make a task-list. It doesn't hurt to overdo it.

You've probably noticed that the 'finish by' column is not filled in. That's because the date by which you want to finish the assignment will depend on how you *interpret* the task-list.

step 3: interpret your task-list

The value of the task-list is that you can now make decisions based on the information it contains.

For example:

- the most important single event (worth 80% of your marketing subject) is a report. Obviously you'll need to dedicate more time to this assessment than an assignment worth only 10%.

- The next most important item is the exam for English Literature. At 70% of the subject mark, it's too risky to try to cram it in an all night effort.

- One of the assessments is a presentation which you have to give the day after the major report is due. You are horrified about giving a presentation, but relax … it only represents 10% of the subject mark.

It's now clear what tasks need to be completed during the semester, and essentially in what order. Some things are immediately apparent. For example late May will be a very difficult time unless some of the assignments are completed in advance.

Allow yourself enough time to prepare for exams. Plan to complete assignments a few days ahead of their due dates. This way you build room into your schedule in case a problem causes you to fall behind.

If you think some of this strategy may seem a little extreme, remember that it is your own time and money that you are investing into study. Athletes, even when competing at a social level, usually approach their sport with a strategy. Study is no different.

finding the time to study

know how you spend your time

An understanding of how you spend your time is fundamental to the art of *finding* time. Many students can increase the amount of time they devote to study merely by being aware of it – in other words, keeping a record of where and when you study. It's quite useful to keep track of what you do with your time during a typical week. For example record the hours spent in classes, at meals, studying, sleeping, socializing, musing, napping, watching TV, working, taking care of kids, lying by the pool – the lot.

How much time did you spend? There are 168 hours in a week. If your total is less than 168 hours, in theory you have a little time to spare. If your total exceeds 168 hours, you're trying to do too much.

how to find 'extra' time

Now that you have a better idea of how you spend your time, you may discover that you need *extra* time. Setting aside study time builds valuable life skills like discipline, time management, and goal setting. If there simply aren't enough hours in a week to fit in all the things you want to do, the trick is to do things differently.

The following suggestions are all good ways to get the best out of the time you have.

 cut down on television

If you sacrifice just one hour of television a day you will free seven hours a week.

 wake up one hour earlier

For many students, waking up any earlier than absolutely necessary would be unthinkable ... but it really is one of the easiest ways of saving time.

When I was studying, cutting down on watching television, and waking up earlier gave me between 20 to 30 *extra* hours a week.

tricks of the trade
You can revise a considerable amount of information by making audio files of the key points, and listening to them in the car.

Remember to be reasonable in your estimations – don't try to be a hero by limiting yourself to four hours of sleep a night.

 use "dead time"

Dead time is time spent waiting in queues, driving, travelling, and so on. Obviously it is difficult to write an essay during this time, or carry out a full scale background research into a topic, but you can revise material for an exam or rehearse material for an in-class presentation.

tricks of the trade
Consider investing in a flashcard program for your phone, or making small pocket sized flashcards that you can easily carry around. Revise while you're waiting at the bus stop, or in a long queue.

 use little 'chunks' of time

It's amazing what you can accomplish in half an hour. Often if you have a break between classes it may seem like it's not worth the effort to start something study related … after all, by the time you start you'll have to pack up. Not so. Even if you manage to write just one paragraph of an essay, its one paragraph less that you have left to do. Many larger tasks are best accomplished step by step.

using the 'extra' time to study

Okay, so now you've found some time to study. Your next challenge is to actually *use* this time to study. The three biggest hurdles will probably be lack of motivation, procrastination and distraction.

motivation

Remaining motivated is an essential element in successful study. It provides the drive to get started, stay focused, and keep going—even when things get tough. Motivation can help you put in consistent effort, overcome setbacks, and perform at your best.

Here are a few ways to remain motivated.

 remind yourself of your goals

Now is the time to remind yourself exactly why you want the qualification you are studying for. Visualise yourself receiving the degree or diploma. Imagine the sort of job you may find as a result of your efforts. It's easier to work hard when you can picture the reward.

 find something interesting

Try to find something interesting about every assignment. Your assignments have been designed with certain learning objectives in mind. Think about how the knowledge you gain will benefit you. It's far easier to spend three hours on something you are interested in, as opposed to something that bores you senseless.

 inspire yourself

Surround yourself with fellow students who are positive and keen – it's amazing what a boost of confidence they can give you at a difficult time.

avoiding procrastination

Procrastination is putting off until later what should really be done now. In some cases this can be almost an art form. Forcing yourself to start is often the hardest part, so here are some tips to help you get moving.

 make the task manageable

If you can cut a big job down in size, even if just a little, it won't seem as daunting. Even completing a paragraph of an essay is a step in the right direction (and one step less for the next day).

 do something ... anything

When it comes to getting started, it doesn't really matter what you do or where you start … as long as you do something. Try reading a chapter of your textbook. If you get stuck, try skimming the table of contents or read the preface. At the very least, just open your textbook and dwell on anything that catches your eye.

Try jotting down random ideas about the topic you are studying, or perhaps write a list of things to do for the assignment. If all else fails, switch to another subject. The chances are that even if you only do a little, you will feel a lot better about your efforts.

> **tricks of the trade**
> Always end the days work with something started so the next day you are not faced with a blank page. Leave the hard (boring etc) parts of the assignment to when you are most alert. Leave the more routine parts for when you are tired.

distractions

Doing something will more often than not get you started. The next trick is to keep going. It's a little like starting a temperamental lawnmower, now that you finally have it running … don't turn it off.

Let's not forget most of you have worked very hard to find some precious time to study. It's important not to waste it. One of the big challenges is avoiding distractions. Here are a few tips:

 use voicemail

My advice is to learn how *not* to use your phone. The best weapon against phone interruptions is to use voicemail. You can always call back at a time that suits you.

 learn how to say "no"

Despite the best of intentions, things have a way of intruding when we are trying to complete assignments or study for an exam. Everybody is going to the movies, or going out, the list is endless. It's not easy, but you have to learn how to say "no" to any *unplanned* activities.

 hide

Sometimes your only option is to hide away. In fact this is often the best option available. Libraries are perfect places to hide. There are no distracting phone calls (make sure to turn your mobile off), no television sets, and no computer games.

There are many excellent books and websites that teach time management, and they are all well worth looking at. Even so, remember the basics: organise yourself, find some time to study, and *use* that time to study. Effective time management will make a great deal of difference to your study efforts, however much of your learning will take place in another environment – the classroom (whether that is in person or online).

3. in class

With most formal education, learning is conducted through a series of lectures, tutorials, or 'classes'. At university lectures and tutorials are separate events, while at many colleges they are bundled together. Lessons can range from fifty minute periods at school to three hour classes at college. Some classes are conducted in-person at the campus, while others are 'virtual classes' online. Whatever the case, attendance and an enthusiastic attitude is a great start.

attendance is the key

Maintaining a good attendance record is vital to successful study, whether online or on-campus. Here are a few compelling reasons why.

personal interaction

Much of what you learn stems from personal interaction with teachers, not textbooks. This applies even to online lectures where the class itself is held in real time over a learning platform such as Zoom.

Your teacher will explain essential terms and give examples. If you don't catch on at first, you have the opportunity to ask questions. This is something you can't do with a textbook or with a friend's notes.

participation

Attending classes gives you the opportunity to participate. You can test your ideas and use the interaction with classmates and teachers to develop confidence as a student.

exam and assignment 'clues'

Teachers tend to highlight the key terms and concepts. Attending classes gives you an opportunity to get inside your teachers' minds to figure out what they consider most important. This helps when you're trying to work out the sort of material that might be included in exams for example. Listen for clues such as your teacher saying, "One of the more important things to understand is …"

value for money

You (or someone in your family) pay for the classes you attend. School fees, course fees, government loan fees … studying is an expensive business. It's an interesting exercise to calculate how much each class is costing you. If you accept the view that "time is money" then it's quite easy to work out the financial value attributed to completing your course.

preparing for class

A lot can be accomplished in terms of study, *before* your class even starts. Here are a few ideas.

 revise previous class notes

Smart students will spend a little time revising their previous notes. If you realise you have not understood something properly, make a note of it, and ask in class.

 preview current topic

Just before class is a good time to gather your thoughts and mentally prepare yourself for the topic. You should always be aware of what your current topic is. If you're not sure, check the unit outline to see what topic or topics will be covered.

If the subject is following a certain textbook you should read the relevant chapter, chapter outline, or summary before class. Familiarity with the topic before class gives you a far greater chance of learning it well.

what to do in class

Whether you are in a virtual or online class environment, or studying in person on-campus, there is a lot you can do 'in-class' that will affect how successful you are as a student.

Here are a few good strategies.

arrive on time

Some teachers have quite a strict policy regarding arrival times, others are very easygoing. Either way, it is good policy to arrive or log in to your class on time. Teachers and students usually notice someone who arrives late, if for no other reason than it disrupts the class. At times being late will be unavoidable – it only becomes a problem if you are *always* late.

position yourself in the classroom

If possible, sit front and centre (and hope everyone else in the class isn't following the same advice). This is generally the best location for listening, asking questions and seeing visual materials. On the other hand, having a chat to the person next to you, sleeping, or reading the newspaper is far more difficult.

The online equivalent to this is turning your camera on. For many classes this is now compulsory, but even if it's not – most teachers really appreciate it.

be alert and attentive

Paying attention in class is very different to when we pay attention to our friends at lunch.

Listening in class should be goal-oriented and purposeful, not passive.

Even though at times your teacher may be doing most or all of the talking, you can still be an alert listener. Your posture and expression contribute greatly to being alert ... it also makes you *look* more alert. This is another compelling reason to have your camera on in online classes.

Listen to others when they speak. Give them eye contact or nod your head when you agree with them. You can be certain that it will be appreciated by your fellow students and your teacher.

 take notes

One important activity that helps not only in staying alert, but with all areas of study is note-taking. It's also known as active listening, and will be covered in greater detail in the next chapter.

 ask questions: participate

There are many excellent reasons to ask questions, not least that you want something answered. However by asking questions, you are also organising the subject matter in your mind. A good question will emphasise your presence to the teacher in a positive way, and if you think about it, it enables you to practice speaking before fellow students and your teacher.

> **tricks of the trade**
> If you are shy and uncomfortable about asking questions, ask something early in the lesson to break the ice. At this stage most teachers are happy to get feedback.

The in-class experience is an important one as it is where much of your learning will take place. It doesn't matter whether your class is online or in person; remember to turn up to class regularly, prepare a little before the class, and remain alert and attentive.

4. taking notes

One of the most common questions students ask in class is "should we write this down?" A standard teacher-like answer is usually, "it's up to you." The answer should probably be a straightforward, "Yes, you *should* write this down."

In fact, it is good policy to have a pen (or iPad or laptop) in hand when carrying out most activities concerned with study. When you're reading a novel for relaxation, or listening to a friend over of cup of coffee, it would be unusual to take notes. But study and learning is different. No one will examine how much information we've retained during our coffee, and then give us a grade on it; but they will do exactly that at school, college or university.

why take notes

Taking notes is a relatively tedious thing to do. So why go to the trouble? There are several compelling reasons.

encourages active listening

Taking notes promotes active listening – the writing is the 'active' part. It helps you focus your attention on the lesson. If you think about it, it's difficult to take notes and daydream at the same time.

helps recall

Notes help you remember the content of lessons. Most students retain very little of the information that is presented during a class. Noting the central ideas and important pieces of information helps you remember them.

useful for exam revision

In many cases, a subject is not based on a specific textbook, rather on the topics studied in class. In these cases your notes become an essential tool for exam revision.

highlights key terms and concepts

Taking notes heightens your awareness of key terms and concepts. Teachers may be the ones lecturing about a specific subject, but you are the one recording what *you* determine to be the main points and key ideas. In this sense, taking notes puts you in charge of your learning.

When taking notes, most of the time it will be from one of two possible sources – notes taken while reading textbooks; or notes taken while listening in class.

taking notes from a spoken source

Taking notes from a spoken source, such as a lecture or your teacher in class, is usually more difficult than taking notes from a textbook because you are restricted by time.

Here are some suggestions that may help:

 always give your notes a heading

It's good practice to always note the name of the subject, teacher and date, at the start of your lesson.

 use cues from the teacher

Perhaps the most important technique in note-taking is learning what is and isn't important to write down. While there are no magic formulas for knowing *exactly* what to write, many teachers will indicate what sections of the lesson are important. For example, they may use a PowerPoint slide with key points on it, or they may simply *tell* you that a section is important. Some teachers will slow their delivery to give you time to write. It is important to be alert and attentive; otherwise you'll miss any cues offered.

 don't attempt to write everything

Do not attempt to write down every word that comes out of the teacher's mouth. Remember, the object of your notes is to be able to recall the *main points* of the lesson, exam information, or information that is relevant to your assessment. If your teacher speaks too quickly, simply ask them to slow down or to repeat something that you missed.

 use abbreviations

It is a good idea to use abbreviations as much as possible. There are many standard ones that can help avoid a sore wrist.

Some useful standard abbreviations include:

>	more / greater than
<	less than
=	the same as
≠	not the same as
e.g.	for example
α	at
w.	with
→	leads to

You can also invent your own abbreviations for words that you know are used often. Try to make them intuitively obvious. For example:

psych.	psychology
mktg.	marketing
advg.	advertising
popl.	population
prom.	promotion

 leave plenty of space

As you take the notes, leave enough room for your comments and anything else you might want to add later. This is something that applies to writing on tablets or laptops.

The next two points are only applicable to taking notes using pen and paper.

 use one side of a sheet of paper

You should aim to take notes only on one side of the page. This has the advantage that you can spread out notes on a table and see what you have, without constantly having to turn over and check.

 write neatly

Try to write neatly. Yes, you may be rushed. Yes, you may be trying to concentrate on what your teacher is saying. But if you cannot read your notes, it will be difficult to study from them.

taking notes from a written source

Taking notes from a textbook, website or any other written source is obviously a lot easier than taking notes from a spoken source. Time pressure is not an issue – you can take as long as you want to make notes. Many techniques are the same as taking class notes; nevertheless, you may be able to use these additional tips.

tricks of the trade

Some students have found colour coding their notes useful – they use coloured paper for the notes taken from journal articles, books etc., but ordinary white paper for notes taken in class.

 note the source

It's very useful to put the source of your notes as a heading. Include some of the major elements that align with one of the standard referencing systems. This could include basic information such as the title of a book, journal or web page, the author, date of publication and the URL if applicable.

 preview before you write

You should try to read the whole chapter, or relevant section, before starting to take notes. It will help you stay focussed on only the points that are of interest to you. The 'preview' part of the PQ4R method (discussed in the next chapter) works very well here.

 understand the structure

Most textbooks have a very similar structure. The opening paragraph of each chapter will usually contain an overview of what will be in that chapter. They also usually have outline or summary sections which can be very useful when taking notes.

decide on a note-taking method

One of the most important decisions concerning note taking is deciding on the method you will use to take them.

This is partly dependent on recognising the teaching style of your teacher and your own learning style. Some teachers have a very structured lesson with each point logically ordered, while others will leave far more time to discussion, and will alter the direction of the lesson depending on the student feedback. Equally, some students prefer to write everything in order as it is presented, while others will try to get an overall grasp of the topic.

The two main note-taking methods are 'outlining' and 'mind-mapping'.

outline format

The 'outline' format is excellent, particularly if the lesson is well structured. Basically this format uses a series of headings and sub-headings. These are usually indented and sometimes numbered.

It's important not to get too carried away with issues such as which numbering system you should use, and how many heading levels are appropriate. The idea is to produce something you can refer back to and understand. So dots or dashes, for example, are fine to mark the various headings.

> **MARKETING**
> - Product
>   - Rational
>   - Emotional
> - Price
> - Place
> - Promotion
>   - Advertising
>   - Sales promotion
>   - Personal selling
>   - Public relations

concept- or mind-mapping

Outlining is linear and organised, but that is not always the way our minds work. Sometimes our minds work like web sites where groups of pages, ideas and concepts are linked together, or even go off on their own into other groupings or webs.

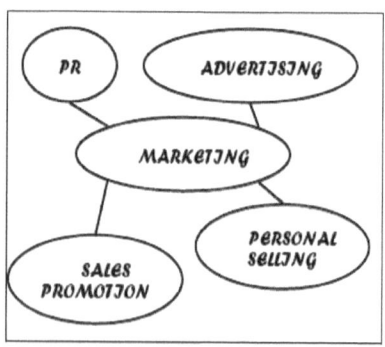

A mind map consists of a key word or symbol surrounded by other key words or concepts that relate to it. The actual pattern or structure the mind map takes is up to you.

For some students, a mind map is more visually appealing than an outlined list. Also the relationships between concepts can be highlighted graphically, often using fewer words. Of course you can choose a combination of all these techniques, depending on your mood, and the nature of the subject being studied.

note taking equipment

There are quite a few items that will make note-taking far easier; some are essential, some are optional. The essential items are, something to write with, and something to write on.

2B or not 2B

Pencils are useful because you can erase and rewrite. Pens create a permanent record. Personally I prefer the humble pencil – a B or 2B, in fact. The hard leads are more difficult to erase, the softer leads are easier to work with. I quite enjoy sharpening the pencil – it gives me a sense of progress … the feeling that I have actually written enough to blunt a pencil.

Colour is another powerful tool when taking notes – something like Textas, highlighters or coloured pencils would work perfectly. Important points could be coloured red, for example.

A4 loose-leaf notebook

Use a loose-leaf notebook of standard dimensions – generally A4. The smaller sizes are too inefficient, and difficult to file. Loose-leaf notebooks have the advantages of allowing you to tear out the pages and file them later.

laptop and tablet computers

Laptop and tablet computers have a number of advantages as a note-taking tool. They enable you to insert missing material at any point without erasing or rewriting. You don't have to worry about your handwriting, and many students can type a lot faster than they can write.

But there are also quite a few disadvantages. Computers are more costly to buy than paper and pencil, and you'll probably need to keep it with you at all times. Also depending on the style of note taking you use, a computer may not be appropriate – for example if you use mind mapping, a computer would be quite cumbersome. And many people are very slow typists.

recorded classes

Many lectures and classes on the major learning platforms such as Moodle, Blackboard will be recorded and made available to students. An alternative is to use a small cassette or digital recorder to record your lectures or classes. Obviously, the big advantage with any recording is that you can stop and start the lesson to take notes.

When you are listening to a recorded class, it is often better to listen to the whole lesson before starting to take notes. It gives you a chance to determine the structure of the lesson, and have an idea as to which are the important sections.

Recorded lectures and classes are a wonderful resource; however, sometimes students stockpile them planning to listen to them at some future date. The result may well be a binge session of dozens of lectures, or simply not watching any at all.

what to do with your notes

use your notes!!

The most important thing about your notes is that you *use* them. You should read your notes and think carefully about what you are reading. If something isn't clear, ask your fellow students, or your teacher. Summarising your own notes into an outline is a great way to learn. Similarly, using your notes to review key points covered in a lesson is an excellent way of revising the material.

don't destroy your notes

Some students take great delight in destroying all their notes at the end of semester. This is not a good idea; it is definitely useful to keep them. You might find your old notes will be very handy for any future studies.

So, as you can see, there is more to note-taking than one would initially think. And, like many things associated with study, practice makes perfect – the more you take notes the better you will get at it. Now that you have a way of getting information down on paper, we will focus on ways of retaining it.

5. retaining information

Retaining information is a skill that takes practice, perseverance, and patience to master. Sometimes your goal is to remember information only for the short term (for example, just until the exam), or in other cases you may want to retain information for a longer time. This chapter will outline a few of the many techniques available for retaining information.

understanding your material: PQ4R

The best way of remembering something is to understand it, and one of the better known techniques for understanding material is the PQ4R method. PQ4R stands for Preview, Question, Read, Reflect, Recite, and Review, a method that is based on the work of educational psychologist Francis P. Robinson. It has also surfaced as SQ3R (Survey, Question, Read, Recite, Review) and quite probably there are other variations as well.

P - preview

Previewing is a little like scouting out the terrain before you formulate a plan of attack. You can preview a chapter of a book, an article, or even an entire book, using features that are already 'built in' – things like the contents page, the preface, the chapter outline or summary.

 ### use the contents page

A good way of previewing a whole book is to start with the contents page. The table of contents is basically an outline allowing you to see at a glance what topics are covered and in what order. It gives you a sense of the structure of the whole book and how the author has arranged the topics as well as how these topics relate to one another.

 ### don't forget the preface

Authors use prefaces to describe their goals and the features of their textbooks. The preface will often describe the organisation of the book. It will explain the purpose of all those multicoloured boxes or learning features, for example. In most prefaces, authors take you through the book step by step.

 ### chapter outline or summary

The best way of previewing the chapter of a book is to look for either a chapter outline or summary, or sometimes both. In some textbooks they are beautifully ordered ready for learning, already in bullet points. Key learning objectives are often highlighted, as are key terms and definitions.

Q - question

It is important to always keep in mind why you want the information you are attempting to retain. Is it for an exam, an assignment, or is it a concept you need to understand before you can progress? In other words, you should be aware of the *questions* you want to answer – there is no point reading aimlessly. I find it useful to actually write the questions down before I begin to read.

1R - read

Once you have phrased questions, in the PQ4R method, you read the material so that you can answer the questions. This method creates a sense of purpose that will help you focus on the key points of the subject matter. As you respond to each question, remember to jot down key words and concepts in your notebook.

💡 *beware of the highlighting pen*

A common technique when reading is to run a highlighting pen through countless paragraphs of your beautiful textbook. Some would argue that textbooks are meant to be used – so what's wrong with highlighting? Besides wrecking your book, it gives the false sense of actually having learnt something by virtue of dragging a brightly coloured line through it. They are definitely very useful, but only when used with purpose – different colours for different concepts, for example.

 use Post It notes

Personally, I like to use Post-It notes. You can buy them in all manner of shapes, sizes and colours. Invest in a variety and liberally stick comments and notes all through your textbook. Bright pink may be exam related, yellow notes might mean 'needs more revision', and blue might be essay related.

2R – reflect

Psychologists and educators have shown that you learn more effectively when you reflect on what you are learning. Reflecting on a subject basically means, thinking about it. For example, if I read about the firing of neurons, one way of understanding it is by thinking of dominoes lined up in such a way that when one falls it knocks the other over, creating a 'chain reaction' of sorts.

3R – recite

Reciting the material is one of the most important factors in the ability to retain information. It involves putting the ideas you have just learned into your own words and saying them out aloud (literally *reciting* it). Studies show that reading, and then reciting material is far more effective than simply reading and re-reading.

 ### talk to yourself!

Actually tell yourself what you have learned. The act of vocalisation is a very powerful way to learn – after all, actors don't learn their lines in silence. Obviously how loud you are will depend on where you are, who's around, and your level of concern over how you think they'll react to you.

 ### teach someone else

Another excellent technique (perhaps one of the best learning techniques) is to teach someone else. Why not explain what you have learned to your mother, brother or sister, or one of your fellow students. An effort to teach something focuses your attention on the subject, really reinforces the information in your memory, and also reveals to you any weak areas of your knowledge … particularly if your chosen 'victim' asks a lot of questions!

4R - review

The process of reviewing is basically testing yourself.

 ### use existing questions

You can use existing questions to test your knowledge. Most textbooks will have review questions at the end of each chapter. The Internet has countless sites that have quizzes and self tests. Perhaps you can even make up a quiz for yourself using many of the excellent flashcard programs that are available.

 find out why

If you don't understand something, try re-reading the relevant section of your textbook. Perhaps you can consult other references which might give you a different perspective. I've often found general references such as encyclopaedias (including Wikipedia) very useful as their articles are well structured and easy to understand.

putting it all together

The PQ4R method is not necessarily a linear process. Your study session may run something like this.

- First, you preview a book by looking at the contents page, and then clarify the questions you want answered.
- Again you preview, however this time a specific chapter.
- Then you look at your questions again, and read a section.
- You have a quick cup of coffee, read some more, think about what you have read, and realise not much has sunk in.

- You look at the question you want to answer again, re-read the section – this time taking notes as you read.
- You think about what you have read.
- Now you close the book and try to recite what you have learned. It's not as much as you had hoped.
- You have another coffee, and then try the quiz at the end of the chapter … a little more luck.
- Back to reading …

Get the idea?

tricks of the trade
If possible, review your notes about half an hour after writing them. Psychologists have found that we forget about half of what we have learned within half an hour.

remembering your material

At some stage in the study process you will have to remember things like formulas, definitions, or a list of items. In this instance, understanding the underlying concept may not be as important as simply being able to apply a formula.

There are quite a few well known memory 'tricks', including chunking, using mnemonic devices, and repetition.

chunking

Chunking is the process of dividing a large task into smaller segments. This is a very useful learning technique, particularly if you have a lot to learn (say, a whole page of formulas). If you can break a large segment into smaller manageable 'chunks' of information the task becomes far easier.

mnemonic devices

A mnemonic device is usually an acronym, jingle, or phrase that represents a chunk of information. Recalling the phrase "Every Good Boy Deserves Fruit" has helped many people remember the musical keys E, G, B, D, F.

Many a science students has used the acronym Roy G. Biv to remember the colours of the rainbow (red, orange, yellow, green, blue, indigo, violet). When studying a neuroscience unit, I used the acronym DRAT to remember Dendrites Receive (impulses) and Axons Transmit (impulses).

use vivid images

It is far better if you can associate an image with what you have to remember, and the more vivid and unusual the image, the better. For example what does the 'boy who deserves fruit', or Roy G Biv look like?

repetition

An excellent method of remembering something is to repeat it. As children we learned the alphabet and multiplication by rote learning, which is essentially repetition. Athletes repeat drills until a certain set of movements becomes second nature. A musician practices chords, or drum beats until they don't even have to think about it.

 summarise and re-summarise

One way of repeating things you have learned is to summarise your class notes, or summarise the chapters of a book. If you summarise the summary, that is a further repetition.

 use flashcards

A technique I have used quite successfully is creating flashcards. One side contains a term or key concept, and the other side is the definition. I used old business cards collected precisely for this purpose.

tricks of the trade
Many instant print companies will give you business cards that they cannot use because of printing errors – these make excellent flashcards.

I would print the terms and definitions on address labels which makes sticking them on to the card very easy. I got the 'repetition effect' firstly by entering the information on the computer, and then by seeing each of the terms and definition as I stuck them onto the cards. I used to carry the cards in my pocket so could test myself anytime.

Of course, this method is very 'old school' compared to the range of flashcard apps and programs that are easily downloaded to your mobile phone or computer.

The more you use the techniques presented in this chapter, the better you will get at them, and the easier they will seem. Remember the three P's: practice, perseverance, and patience.

6. written assignments

Most of your classes or courses will have some kind of assessment task which contributes to your final mark. In many cases that task is a written assignment, essay or report. The term 'written assignment' is usually generic and can refer to essays, research papers, reports, and so on. While the terms are often interchangeable, there is a difference between essays and reports.

A report usually informs the reader simply and objectively about all relevant issues. Reports have three common features: a pre-defined structure, independent sections, and reaching unbiased conclusions. Essays don't always have separate sections, and typically involve constructing a debate around different arguments in favour of, or not in favour of a particular issue.

This chapter looks at the process of completing good written assignments, from initially understanding the task, to final presentation and layout.

understanding the task

The first step in the process of completing a written assignment is to understand the task.

Examine what you have to do in detail before you start.

 ### check the assignment guide

Usually most major assignments will have a set of guidelines or instructions – an assignment guide. Make sure you read it before you start. If anything is unclear, this is the time to ask your teacher.

 ### understand the scope

Understand the scope of the assignment. Is it a major assignment, or a relatively small one? How long is the assignment meant to be? Is it primarily meant to be your own ideas, or are your required to read certain references. If so, are there any particular references you need to consult?

 ### identify the key terms used

The following are some common terms used in both exam questions and written assignment guidelines.

Analyse: Examine in very close detail; identify important points and main features.

Comment on: Identify and write about the main issues, giving your reactions based upon what you have read or heard in class.

Compare: Show how two or more things are similar. Indicate the relevance or consequences of these similarities.

Contrast: Set two or more items or arguments in opposition and point out the differences. Indicate whether the differences are significant.

Critically evaluate: Weight arguments for and against something, assessing the strength of the evidence on both sides.

Define: Give the exact meaning of. Where relevant, show that you understand why the definition may be problematic.

Describe: Give the main characteristics or features of something, or outline the main events.

Discuss: Write about the most important aspects of; give arguments for and against; consider the implications of.

Evaluate: Assess the worth, importance or usefulness of something, using evidence. There will probably be cases to be made for both for and against.

Examine: Put the subject under the microscope, looking at it in detail.

Explain: Make clear why something happens, or why something is the way it is.

Illustrate: Make something clear and explicit, giving examples or evidence.

Outline: Give only the main points, showing the main structure.

 read the rubric

A rubric is a scoring guide used to evaluate and assess your work based on a set of clearly defined criteria. It outlines what is expected in an assignment and how it will be graded. The obvious point is, make sure you set your sights on at least a pass.

tricks of the trade
Highlight the relevant parts of the rubric that will ensure you get the marks you are aiming for. Then cut and paste them into the first draft of your assessment as a guide.

gathering information

You can get information for an essay, report or any assessment from your own knowledge and experience; but generally this is not what will be required. Most reports will require you to investigate something (perhaps interview people, experiment, gather data), report on your findings and give your own opinion *backed up by the opinion of others*. So, at some stage you will need to consult references such as textbooks, reference works, web sites, journals, diaries, or professional reports.

conducting your own research

Conducting your own research via interviews or surveys is an excellent way to learn, however it is very time consuming. It would only be expected for you to do this if it was a specific requirement of a subject. Your report will probably only include the summary of your findings; you should place the original questionnaires, transcripts of interviews or any other details in a section called the Appendix (discussed later in this chapter).

books and journals

In some cases you will rely on your textbook to complete a report, but generally your teacher will expect you to read a variety of books and journals. The majority of journals will be found in online databases

> **tricks of the trade**
> Familiarise yourself with the databases that will be relevant to your studies. Make sure you know how to access them, and use the search functions to your best advantage.

Most academic databases are only available through subscription. One of the advantages of being affiliated with an educational institution is that you will have access to their subscription. The library will be of great help here – most librarians will be happy to help you find the references you need.

online resources

The Internet is an exceptionally powerful and efficient research tool … as long as you know how to look for things. A good strategy for searching online starts with clearly defining what you're looking for and using specific, focused keywords.

> ***tricks of the trade***
> Begin with a simple search, then refine it using tools like quotation marks for exact phrases, site-specific searches, and filters for date or file type.

Evaluate sources critically by checking for the reliability, authorship, and recency of the information. If the results of your search aren't helpful, don't hesitate to reword your search or try different terms.

referencing

Now that you've gathered your information, if you're going to use it, you need to let the reader know where it came from. This is called referencing. There are so many variations when it comes to referencing that even seasoned academics often disagree. Each academic institution will have its preferred method.

Harvard referencing is often used as a generic term for author–date citation styles, but it is not a single, fixed system. There are many types of 'Harvard referencing'.

The important concept to understand with any system is that there are *two* parts to an academic reference: the references at the end of your assessment and the in-text citations, which are used throughout the assessment itself.

how to reference in-text

An in-text reference is an acknowledgement of your source material placed *within* the assessment – in fact at the exact point where you are using some else's words or ideas. It is usually an abbreviated form of the reference – the full reference will appear at the end of the document in a 'references section'.

The two major styles of referencing are APA (American Psychological Association), and MLA (Modern Language Association). APA is commonly used in the social sciences (such as psychology, education, sociology), and emphasises the author and date of publication in in-text citations. For example: (Smith, 2020). MLA is often used in the humanities, particularly in literature, arts, and cultural studies. It focuses on the author and page number in in-text citations. For example: (Smith 45)

Some colleges or individual teachers may have a preference for a particular referencing style, but whichever system you use, it's important to remain consistent throughout your report.

Sometimes you will be using an idea or a general concept from an information source there is no need to include a page number. But if you are quoting directly or referring to a specific part of a book or article, you will need to include the page number.

Here are some examples:

The first theory of market fluctuation was proposed in 1934 (Hamilton 1994, p. 58).

Or:

Hamilton (1994, p. 58) states that the first theory of market fluctuation was proposed in 1934.

There are also countless books, guides and websites that can help you with referencing. Your academic institution will no doubt it's own guidelines. It's an excellent investment of your time to learn the basics well.

works cited, references, bibliography

There is a certain level of confusion between the nature of a *references* page, a *bibliography*, and *works cited* list. In most cases your teacher will be happy if you use *any* of the three terms for a page that lists the books, journal articles and websites you have referred to in your assignment. If you used a source as part of your research, but didn't quote, paraphrase, or refer to it, it does not go in the list.

Traditionally a bibliography referred only to books (*biblio* being the Greek for 'book') and journals. Most students now will use mainly online sources so the standard title is usually References.

how to format a reference page

The References section appears at the end of the report.

Each reference is listed alphabetically according to the surname of the author. This is followed by the author's first name, the year of publication, the book title (in italics), and then the publisher. For example:

> Stanton, William J., Miller, Kenneth E., Layton, Roger A. (1994). *Fundamentals of Marketing, Third Australian Edition*. McGraw-Hill

It's not much different for a journal or magazine article, except instead of book title, you list the title of the article, the name of the journal, the volume number, and the pages. The name of the journal is in italics, while the title of the article is placed within inverted commas.

> Smith, Fred J., (2003). "Guerrilla Marketing", *Business Review Weekly*. Oct. 2023, 27(5) pp 122-128

The referencing for an item found on the Internet is similar to that of a book, only you include the web address (the full URL, not just the website) and the date you accessed it. For example:

Macdonald, Emma (1996) 'Brand Awareness as an Indication of Advertising Effectiveness'. *Marketing Research On-Line*, [*Electronic version*], http://www.economics.com/Hamilton.html Retrieved on 04 July 2024.

Each referencing system will have a slightly different way of formatting the elements, but the elements themselves are fairly universal.

why reference your material

Referencing is an essential part of learning to write a good assessment. Referencing your work backs up and supports the points you make, and allows the reader to verify your sources of information. It also shows what parts of the report are your original ideas.

 backs up your points

Indicating where you obtained your information will help build your argument. Depending on the status of the reference you have used (a well known authority on a subject, for example), your references will support a particular point you are making.

 verifies your sources

References make your work verifiable. If the reader is interested in a particular aspect of the report, or would like more information on something you have commented on, the reference will help them find the original source.

 avoids plagiarism

If you purposely use and do not acknowledge materials from published or other sources, this can constitute plagiarism. This includes copying from another student's essay or simply 'cutting and pasting' from an online source. Plagiarism is a serious issue at tertiary level and can be a sufficient basis for the recording of a failure in a subject or even expulsion from a course.

At the undergraduate level, it cannot be expected that all your ideas and views will be original. Much of what you think, say and write will have appeared somewhere in print before. So don't hide your sources – for most teachers the fact that you have consulted other books and authors is a good thing.

writing drafts

Just how many drafts are needed will vary. It depends on the complexity of the topic and the amount of effort you are willing to put in. For some students the first draft is the *only* draft! At the very least you should aim to have one draft and one revision. Think of the first draft as simply a way of getting your ideas on paper no matter how 'rough' they may be.

fill the screen with writing

Even though it seems so easy, many students have trouble with initially getting words onto the computer.

Here are some tips to help you start writing.

 write out the question

It helps to review exactly what the assignment is asking you to do, then write it down. If the question has several parts break it up in your document so each section is clear – this will help greatly in structuring your report.

 write what you know

Skim through the material you have gathered, and try to answer the questions you have just written … in your own words. It doesn't matter if what you write is not grammatically correct. For example:

The history of psychology can be traced back to the Ancient Greeks ??? Aristotle? Plato (not sure which? – check). However, the father of modern psychology is usually credited ??? as Wilhelm Wundt (check spelling.).

As you can see, you can pepper the writing with notes to yourself.

 don't edit yourself … yet

Do not revise as you write, or correct spelling, punctuation, etc. Just write, write, and write some more. This is the first draft, so what you put down will be revised and organised later. The main task at this stage is to build up your word count.

back up everything

 use 'save as' regularly

By using the 'save as' function of your word processor, you build up a collection of different versions of your document. Each time you save give the file a different name (Report01, Report02, for example).

I usually use 'save as' just before making *major* changes to the document. If I don't like what I have done, it is easy to simply open the previous document, and start again. When your report has been marked and handed back to you, archive all the various versions keeping only the final one for reference.

 back-up your data regularly

It's extremely important to keep a back-up of all your data. There are many methods to achieve this, but I use an external hard drive, and back up all the data on my computer once a week. Even if it's the worst case scenario and my hard drive is wrecked, I would only be losing one week's worth of work. For very important documents or assessments, back up more regularly.

revising the drafts

There are three factors you need to consider when revising your first draft: the content of the assessment, the structure of the assessment and your writing technique.

content

 stick to the point

'Waffling' is writing about things not relevant to the aims of the assignment (highly technical term, isn't it?). This is putting down everything you know simply to get more words on paper. It's acceptable when writing the *first* draft, but now is the time to cut anything that strays from your topic.

 don't write too little

When there is a suggested word limit to your assignment, it's usually an indication of how detailed your analysis needs to be. If you find you don't have enough content, then it's probably an indication that you haven't looked at the various concepts in enough depth, or perhaps you need to develop a few more arguments.

 don't write too much

Beware also of overwriting. Most assignments have a word limit, so make sure you stick to it. The standard leniency is plus or minus 10% of the suggested length; so a 1000 word essay can be between 900 and 1100 words.

structure

 use the outline function

Microsoft Word (and probably most other word processing programs) has an outline function. It is a very practical function and well worth the effort to master. You can attach a selected font to your document heading levels, and if you decide to change the font, you change all the headings in one go.

> **tricks of the trade**
> The outline function is one of the most powerful and probably most under-utilised features in Microsoft Word. It's a great investment of your time to learn how to use it.

More importantly, you can see an outline of the main headings on a single page. Using 'outline', you can also move the headings (and all the text under them) without using 'cut and paste'. This alone is a huge bonus.

 introduction, body and conclusion

Most reports have an introduction, a main body, and a conclusion. The exact nature of the main body will of course depend on the topic. In a long, complex report, the introduction and conclusion will probably have their own sections. In a short report, each may be only a paragraph.

In the introduction you tell us what the report is about and why you are writing it. It is a good place to state definitions. The conclusion should indicate how you have achieved what you stated in the introduction – so the introduction and conclusion should agree with each other.

 use an appendix

The appendix is where you put information that would be too long or involved in the body of the report (and perhaps be distracting to the reader), but nonetheless is important to include. For example, original articles that you have summarised in the report, raw data, questionnaires, transcripts of interviews, lengthy background material, and so on.

technique

 check spelling and grammar

Many words are spelt correctly but are completely wrong in the context of what you are writing. For example "too ducks flu away" is correct according to my spell checker! A computer spell checker is far from perfect. Make sure you check doubtful words with a dictionary.

Turn on all the spelling and grammar checks built into your word processor. Most programs will indicate spelling mistakes with a red line under a word, and a green line under a grammatical error (a click of the mouse will indicate what the error is). By simply trying to get rid of the red and green lines, you will most likely improve your spelling and grammar.

 sentences and paragraphs

Every sentence should basically reflect one idea. As soon as you move onto a new idea, use a new sentence. It can be very frustrating for the reader to decipher a long convoluted sentence. Paragraphs should be one cluster of related points. Much like sentences, you're your paragraphs short and readable. As a general rule, if you see a whole page without a break, the paragraph is too long.

 use headings and sub-headings

Headings and sub-headings help the reader navigate through your report. In longer reports they are absolutely essential. As you can see with this book, the headings help break up large slabs of text, and are usually appreciated by readers.

 back up your points

When you make a point or reach a conclusion, you should have the evidence to justify it. For instance you may use a quote from a textbook, a relevant example, or the opinion of an expert. Merely presenting your own opinion because that's simply "what I think", is generally not enough. Always ask yourself, "On what basis am I making that point?"

presentation and layout

Many schools, faculties or subject disciplines (like science or law, for example) will have very specific guidelines as to how assessments should be presented. If not, what follows should be fairly useful (albeit generic) guide.

general presentation

Some assessments (but certainly not all) will require a title page. This doesn't have to be an elaborate artwork, simply a page indicating the assignment title, your name, the due date, teacher's name and subject or unit, and the name of the academic institution. This is usually centred, often about a third of the way down the page.

Most reports will also have a reference page, and for longer reports, a table of contents and an appendix. In some case an abstract (which is essentially an overview) is required at the start.

layout and formatting

The standard page size is generally A4, with 1 inch (2.54 cm) margins on all sides (top, bottom, left, right). The most common font is Times New Roman, 12-point font. Generally Arial is a good font for headings and subheading, but some faculties prefer a uniform font throughout.

Academic reports are usually double-spaced (including references), with no extra spaces between paragraphs. You should indent first line of each paragraph (usually 0.5 inch or 1.27 cm), and the paragraph should be left-aligned (not justified) for better readability.

Page numbers, should usually be in the top-right corner. Begin with page 1 (after title page, if used). There is no real need to use numbering for the headings. That is usually reserved for legal and scientific documents. One common alternative is to number only the main headings.

tricks of the trade
Use one assignment as a template for all the others. This means you only need to set up your document margins, headings, fonts and general layout only once.

graphs, charts and pictures

Tables, charts, graphs and pictures can be useful to illustrate main points, and to break up the monotony of large slabs of type. Make sure the graphs and various illustrations you use are relevant to the assignment.

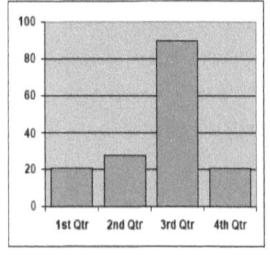

In most word processing programs, the paragraph will wrap neatly around your graph (as in this paragraph). If you're experienced in using a word processor, a task like this will be easy.

There are so many excellent books, websites and videos dedicated solely to every aspect of academic writing, including layout and formatting. Similarly, there are books and websites devoted to referencing alone. Resources such as these are well worth consulting, but remember, (as with so much of the study process) your best teacher is practice. The more essays and reports you write, the better you'll get at it … that's why completing your *first* major written assignment is often the hardest.

7. exams

Sitting exams can be one of the most stress inducing activities for many students. In any given exam, you have a limited amount of time to show what you have learned by answering a set number of questions.

To succeed in exams, it helps if you know about the nature of exams you are likely to encounter, some common types of questions, how to deal with them, and what to do before during and after the exam.

types of exams

There are essentially two types of exams you might encounter: internal and external exams.

Internal (in-class) exams

Internal exams are definitely the most 'user friendly'. They are usually set by your teacher and marked by your teacher. This means (if you're lucky), your teacher may give you those handy clues towards the end of the semester. You will sit these exams in class, most often towards the end of the semester.

tricks of the trade
Make sure you don't miss the class where your teacher gives you those handy clues!

External (major) exams

External exams are set externally, in other words *not* by your teacher. The exam dates are set well in advance by the various departments and faculties and quite often even the marking is external.

types of exam questions

There are many different types of exam questions but the most common are multiple choice, short answer and essay questions.

multiple-choice questions

Multiple-choice tests are extremely popular. Teachers like to use them because the grading is objective, and they can be graded quickly and mechanically. Also a well designed multiple choice test can be quite challenging for students. Students like multiple choice, because there is a statistical chance that even with very little preparation, a correct answer might be found.

Easy multiple-choice questions often have *distracters* – answers that seem obviously incorrect. Harder questions have *plausible distracters* – this is an incorrect answer that seems correct. It becomes even harder still with variables such as the "none of the above" or "all of the above" options, or qualifications such as "both (a) and (b), and so on.

There is no substitute for knowing you have the correct answer because of good exam preparation. However if you are not 100% sure of the answer, here are a few tips that may help.

 beware of trick questions

Be suspicious if the right answer 'pops out' at you. Be especially suspicious when it's choice (a). Trick questions often have partly correct answers as early distracters.

 consider every possible answer

Make sure you read through every alternative. After all, the last choice may read "all of the above."

 eliminate wrong answers first

Eliminate answers that you know are incorrect. Read all choices. If you have enough time, find a reason for eliminating each and every answer until you have only one left (hopefully the *correct* one!).

 'absolute' terms are often wrong

Look out for words such as "all", "completely", "never", "always", and "only". Because these words are 'absolute' terms, and they frequently indicate incorrect answers. On the other hand, words such as "usually", "sometimes", "frequently", "probably", and "often" are more likely to indicate correct choices.

 check the grammar

Check that the answer you are choosing makes grammatical sense. The opening part of the question plus your answer should read as a sentence. If it doesn't, check whether other possibilities read as sentences.

 look for similar answers

Look for answers that are very similar to each other. Often one of them is likely to be the correct answer.

 first hunch isn't always best

Change answers when you realise that you have made a mistake or you find another choice that looks more correct. It's only a myth that you should always go with your first hunch.

short-answer or sentence completion

These items ask for a brief response to a question or present a sentence with a blank space that needs to be filled in. They are harder than multiple choice because if you don't know the answer, you're stuck. On the other hand, there are no distracters to lead you astray. If you are *really* stuck, here are a few tips that might help:

scan the whole exam paper

Sometimes the term you may be looking for is used in another part of the test. Scan through the exam paper to see if anything jogs your memory.

 look at the 'article' before the blank

If the article 'a' is used before the blank space, the answer probably begins with a consonant. If the article 'an' is used, the answer probably begins with a vowel.

essay questions

Essay questions require you to produce written responses to questions. Most essays vary in length from a few paragraphs to several pages. They are difficult and time-consuming to mark and often depend on the subjective opinion of the marker. Exams that consist only of writing long complex essays are becoming far less frequent.

tricks of the trade
If you are sitting any exam that requires handwriting, make sure your writing is legible and clear. A marker cannot mark something they cannot read!

Many of the techniques that are used in writing reports are also used in writing exam essays – the key differences are limited time, and your lack of access to any reference information. Here are some points to consider when tackling essay style exam questions.

answer the question

The first step in writing an essay is making certain that you understand the question. So read the question very carefully. Once you feel you *understand* the question ... answer it!

Many students make the mistake of thinking, "the more I write; the better my mark." Writing down everything you know about a subject is not a way to get good marks. If someone asks you "What type of car do you drive?" they don't expect to be given a history of automotive industry starting with the Model-T Ford.

identify the question

Don't waste time copying out the examination question word for word in your answer book, but *do* make sure that you put the question number at the beginning of each answer so it's easy for the marker to see which question (or which part of the question) you are answering.

introductions and conclusions

There are different points of view as to whether you should include elaborate introductions and conclusions or just get to the business of answering the question. The argument against is that teachers don't always have time to read it, and it takes writing time away from you. The argument for is that they establish where you're going and where you've been, and ultimately makes the markers job easier. Let's take the middle road by recommending a *brief* introduction and a *brief* conclusion or summary statement.

 strongest ideas first

After your introduction, express your strongest ideas first. When you lead with the things you know the most about, you convey a good first impression. It is easy for markers to become very tired when confronted with dozens or even hundreds of essays, so give them your best material first. If they are satisfied that you are in control of the essay, they may skim the remainder.

 plan your answers - show your plan

Plan your answers in outline form before you start to write. Careful thought about what you want to say and the order you wish to say it will probably generate more marks than reams of disorganised writing. Plot out the answers in the order that the points occur to you, and then reorder them logically.

One method for incorporating the outline into the essay is to use the left-side pages for outline / draft material and the right-side pages for the final answer. Just make sure you let the marker know that's what you are doing. Most markers will be impressed by the fact that you actually prepared a plan.

 use headings and sub-headings

In longer answers, don't be scared to use headings and sub-headings. Not only does it make marking easier, but it conveys the impression of an exceptionally organised student.

before the exam

be prepared

One of the most important factors that will determine your exam performance is how well you have prepared. If you've been following the suggestions in this book, have planned your study time effectively, attended class regularly, taken good notes and made a real effort to retain information … you have completed most of the steps needed for successful exam preparation.

Other tips include:

 review past exam papers

Past exam papers are valuable sources of information. They indicate the style of questions that you might encounter and give you ideas about the topics covered. Be careful of accessing the past papers too early – you might find questions that seem to make little sense or which you cannot answer. It is probable that you have not yet covered that topic, so do not worry.

 ask your teacher

Don't be scared to ask your teacher about exam questions, especially if it is an in-class exam written by them. Often they can save you countless hours of wasted revision by telling what *won't* be in the exam.

 don't miss revision lessons

It's surprising how many students miss the revision lessons where the teacher's express aim is to try and help you through the exam.

 take extra notice of 'sample' papers

In some cases your teachers will give you sample exams. It goes without saying that you should practice them. Many teachers reward students who practice the sample exams by using some of these questions in the final exam.

avoid self-defeating thoughts

"I hate exams," "I never do well in exams." Does that sound familiar? These negative statements will only reinforce your fears. Feeling nervous before any exam is natural, and in many ways helps you perform at your peak. Excessive nervousness will get in the way, and you should look into various relaxation methods to help you. Anxiety about exams is a frustrating problem, but if you've prepared well, you'll have nothing to worry about.

immediately before the exam

The time just before the exam is important, and there is much you can do to give yourself a better chance of success.

 correct date time and place

A few days before the exam, check to make sure that the time and place you have in your diary are correct, and ensure also that you know exactly where the examination room is.

 check your clock; check your car

In other words, make sure an avoidable technicality doesn't stop you from getting to the exam. For example, make sure that you set your alarm clock so that you don't sleep in ... and be certain your car has enough petrol.

 get a good night's sleep

Get a good night's sleep the night before the exam. This is particularly important for part-time students who may well be working all day before the exam.

get there early

You should get there early, about half an hour to an hour before the start of the exam. If the campus has a coffee lounge, have a coffee or refreshment, and try to relax. There is no harm in skimming over notes, but frantic last minute study is rarely effective.

don't chat too much with others

If possible try to keep to yourself before the exam. Remember, test anxiety is contagious. The last thing you want to hear from a fellow students is, "You mean you didn't study chapter 5!" this will only send you into an unnecessary panic.

the exam kit

There are some items that are essential in almost any exam. Make sure you have an exam 'kit' to take in with you. Here are some things you can include:

- Sharpened 2B pencils, an eraser, and a sharpener.
- Pens – generally blue or black.
- A highlighting pen.
- Tissues, cough lozenges or anything else you can think of.
- Spare batteries for your calculator (if calculators are required).

- A watch. You want to keep track of time just in case there isn't a clock in the exam room (highly unlikely).

food

Don't go to the exam with an empty stomach. Being hungry is distracting, and your brain needs food to function. Don't go into an exam with an overly full stomach. When you eat a large meal, your body redirects blood to your digestive system rather than your brain.

tricks of the trade
When I sat for exams, I would bring a small bottle of water, and one small bite sized chocolate bar for each hour of the exam. Naturally, healthier alternatives are also fine.

cramming

Cramming is useful in emergencies; but it has to be stressed that it is a last resort, and certainly not what exam preparation is all about. Some students mistakenly think that cramming is the same as exam preparation. Think again: one is good careful *preparation*; the other is *desperation*.

 be selective

Only concentrate on those items that will get you the maximum amount of marks. At this stage, don't try to study 'everything. If you are cramming, the best you are hoping for is a pass, and anything better than that is a bonus.

 prioritise

You should allocate the most time to your weaker subjects. It's better to get two passes than a fail and a distinction.

during the exam

Naturally, it's what you do during the exam that counts. Here are some more helpful hints.

 follow the directions!

If you are asked to use black or blue pen, use black or blue pen. Always write your name on the paper. If you are told to circle the letter that indicates the correct choice, do not circle the entire statement or answer. In other words read all the instructions carefully and follow the directions.

 use the 'reading time' wisely

Normally you will be given 10 minutes reading time in addition to the time set for the exam. This is a good time to get a feel for the exam. In exams where there is a choice of which question to answer – the reading time is a good time to start deciding.

💡 spelling and neatness

Students often ask whether spelling and neatness counts. The answer is 'yes'. Essay questions are graded more subjectively than short-answer items, even when markers try to be objective. So, the general impression you make on the marker counts. It's very simple ... if your markers can't read or understand your exam, they can't mark it.

💡 pace yourself

You should work out how many minutes you can allocate to each question. For example in a two hour exam (120 minutes) worth 100 marks, you have 12 minutes for every 10 marks. You can finish a section quicker than planned, but never spend *more* than the planned time on a question.

💡 tackle easy questions first

Try to complete the easier questions (or questions that you can answer well) first. It will give you a sense of confidence, and get you started. Often the process of writing helps the answers spring to mind.

💡 don't panic; move on

If you blank out and cannot remember anything – don't panic. Take a deep breath and relax. If nothing comes to mind, move on to the next question. Don't waste valuable time lingering on a question you don't know. You can always come back to it later.

check and double-check

When you finish the exam with time to spare, resist the urge to leave as soon as you have completed all the items. Instead, make sure you have answered all the questions. There is no harm in double-checking your answers.

after the exam

After you leave the examination room it is tempting to stand around outside and ask others how they went. Don't get too worried at this point about an exam that is now in the past. Your main objective now is to forget about the exam, and either start preparing for the next one, or relax and enjoy the feeling of completion!

8. the psychology of study

Being a good student is a combination of good technique and good attitude. As mentioned in the opening chapter of this book, motivation and the desire to achieve something is a very important factor determining your success as a student. However sometimes, even with the best of intentions, there are obstacles.

setting grade goals

In any graded subject, it's only natural that most students will want the highest possible grade. But sometimes the goal of getting the best grade *at all costs* is actually counter-productive.

As a teacher I often see students drop out of courses because they are not living up their own extremely high expectations of themselves. Comments like "I *never* get a mark below a distinction" are worrying. These students may not progress to the next level of study because anything less than a distinction grade is unacceptable. There is nothing wrong with wanting to do your best, but setting too high a goal can often lead to frustration and stress. Here are some other points to consider.

set your own goals

Make sure the goals you are striving for are your own, and not someone else's. Most students already put enough pressure on themselves without having to live up to the added pressure of others. It helps to remember that while your family or loved ones will have your best interest at heart; it is *you* that has to do the work.

 be realistic

Not all subjects were created equal; not all semesters were created equal. Some will seem quite effortless while others will be gruelling. Some semesters will have a combination of very theoretical subjects with many long essays, while other semesters will have very practical subjects with major exams. Your performance will vary greatly depending on a multitude of factors including everything from your health, social life, or work commitments, to your level of interest in the subjects. The important point is to be realistic about your expectations.

coping with 'difficult' subjects

In any course of study, there will always be some subjects that are simply not as interesting as others, or are just plain difficult. In fact, you may be convinced that some subjects were included in the syllabus solely to torture unsuspecting students (in my case, second year statistics springs to mind). Strangely, these subjects are always compulsory – never electives.

The principles discussed throughout this book will no doubt help you master even the toughest of subjects, but here are a few extra tips that may help.

find something interesting

Rather than simply think, "I hate this subject," find something interesting about it. Often your attitude to the subject may change as you go along.

make it a challenge to succeed

The harder a subject is, the more challenging it is to succeed. Just think about what an achievement it will be to pass a difficult subject that has a very high fail rate.

a step towards your goal

If all else fails, remind yourself that passing each subject is important. Connect it to your eventual goal of getting your qualifications, or landing the job you have always wanted.

dealing with stress

Stress, up to a certain point, is not a bad thing. In fact it can cause you to work harder and concentrate more and so can be beneficial. But as stress increases, it reduces our effectiveness. Dealing with stress is about recognising at what level it begins to have a negative effect. The key is to make use of stress in a positive way. Here are some strategies that may help in managing study related stress.

 gain perspective

Often by looking at things from a different perspective you see that what you were stressing about really isn't that major.

 talk to your teacher

If you have any issues or concerns related to your subject, it is important to approach your teacher first. Some issues arise out of a misunderstanding or simply lack of communication, and are easily solved with a face-to-face meeting.

 do one thing at a time

You can only do one thing at a time. Don't overwhelm yourself by worrying about your *entire* workload. Handle each task as it comes, or selectively deal with matters in order of importance.

 cut extra commitments

Reduce the number of events going on in your life and you have a good chance of staying afloat. For example you may have to give up a few social activities (unthinkable, I know)!

 rest and activity

Make sure sleep isn't what you sacrifice, to get an assignment in on time. It's a vicious cycle: lack of sleep creates stress, and stress stops you from sleeping. Work off stress with physical activity such as going to the gym or a game of social tennis.

support networks

If the pressure of study starts to interfere with your normal functioning (you're depressed, or you can't sleep) then it's important you are able to talk to someone.

trained professionals

You can often get much needed support from trained professionals such as doctors, psychologists or counsellors. Most educational institutions have excellent counselling and advisory services. Don't be embarrassed or hesitant to use them – that's exactly what they are there for.

your fellow students

Some of the friends you make while studying may remain friends (socially and professionally) for a long time. Certainly, during periods of stress, many students have said the only thing that kept them motivated was the support received from their fellow students.

It is not a bad idea to exchange contact details with a student who will be willing to become your 'study-partner' for the semester. Essentially they would collect notes and keep you informed of any events in case you miss a class. The relationship should be mutual – you in turn would do the same for them.

tricks of the trade
Beware of a study-partner who never attends class, and expects you to complete the subject for them.

your family and friends

In most cases, your family and friends will play an important role in your 'academic life'. Perhaps more than anything else, it's vital that they're supportive and understanding.

Communication is the key; let your family and friends know all about what your study involves. Tell them about what you are trying to achieve, and the way you are going to achieve it. Be prepared to compromise. Study is usually at the expense of family time, so understanding is important … from both sides.

determination and persistence

Determination and persistence are two of the most valuable qualities you can develop. While intelligence and talent may offer a head start, it's the steady commitment to keep going - especially through challenges, setbacks, and moments of doubt - that truly leads to success. Every page studied, every problem solved, and every late-night effort adds up over time. Even when progress feels slow, you will build not only knowledge but resilience and confidence. In the long run, it is this quiet, consistent effort that shapes both academic achievement and personal growth.

There are many rewards to successful study: personal growth, a sense of achievement, self-confidence, academic and professional development, to name a few. For many, embarking on a course of study will provide enduring and often life-changing benefits.

references

Cotrell, Stella. 1999. *The Study Skills Handbook*. Palgrave: Hampshire UK

De Fazio, Teresa. 2002. *Studying Part Time Without Stress*. Allen & Unwin: Sydney

Howe, Wally. 1994. *Life's Little Study Tips*. Hale & Iremonger: Sydney

Macqueen Chris, 1998, *Getting ahead in tertiary Study: A practical guide for Business, social science and arts students*. UNSW Press: Sydney

Williams, Lauren, and Germov, John. 2001. *Surviving First Year Uni*. Allen & Unwin. Sydney

Mind mapping was developed by Tony Buzan. Information about mind mapping used in Chapter 4 (Taking notes) was sourced from a website on creative thinking, (www.ozemail.com.au /~caveman /Creative /Mindmap /index.html)

www.ingramcontent.com/pod-product-compliance
Lightning Source LLC
Chambersburg PA
CBHW031426290426
44110CB00011B/546